Gallery Books
Editor Peter Fallon

LISTENING TO BACH

Pearse Hutchinson

LISTENING TO BACH

Gallery Books

Listening to Bach
is first published
simultaneously in paperback
and in a clothbound edition
on 27 March 2014.

The Gallery Press
Loughcrew
Oldcastle
County Meath
Ireland

www.gallerypress.com

ISBN 978 1 85235 596 8 *paperback*
978 1 85235 597 5 *clothbound*

A CIP catalogue record for this book
is available from the British Library.

the arts council
an chomhairle ealaíon
funding literature
artscouncil.ie

Contents

He donat la meva vida al amor dels amics.

I've given my life to the love of friends.

But For Her

On very cold nights when I was a child in bed
he took my feet between his hands to warm them,
believing warm feet kept all the body warm,
and it worked and I slept through the cold.

Out for walks, when I got tired,
he carried me on his back.
What age was I when, walking along the canal,
approaching Latouche Bridge,
I stopped, looked up at him and said:

'Carry, Daddy, carry!'
and he leant down to take me up
but she put a stop to it
looking down at me, decreeing:
'You're too big now to be carried.'

What age was I before that, when,
standing on a traffic island
in the middle of O'Connell Bridge,
holding her hand, waiting to cross,
I looked up at her and said:
'Mammy, I only want you.'

That began to stop when, at fifteen,
I discovered sex,
and went on stopping when, at seventeen,
I discovered booze.

Years later she told me, bitterly:
'I put my hands under your feet.'

But for her, often enough,
we might have gone hungry,
me an' him.

Anna Bligh

Anna Bligh, Premier of Queensland,
speaking to her fellow citizens
on the brink of a great storm:

'Grab each other and get
to a place of safety,
remember that people are irreplaceable.'

Listening, I'm back in my early twenties
standing in the middle of the kitchen
squaring up to my mother

who's just, her eyes mastering mine,
told me, bitter and sad:
'Nobody is irreplaceable.'

I know at once she's wrong, know it
with every fibre of my being.
I'm shocked that she should think that

and tell her so, angrily:
'Nobody is re-placeable'
and fling myself out of the house.

My father knows nothing of all this hurt,
he's already in his refuge —
the back garden, tending the fruit.

Priest and Car, 1969

A tall, thin priest, well over six foot, complete with biretta and ankle-length soutane is walking slowly along one of those calm, broad, pale-grey footpaths which are one of the glories of Barcelona's finest boulevard, the Paseo de Gracia (as it was called then, though not by all), reading his breviary.

On his left are three or four parked cars, shiny but undistinguished, the avant-garde of a new and blasphemous campaign. He ignores them — he still has the centre all to himself.

A car moves slowly along the footpath, directly behind the priest. This goes on for perhaps three or four minutes. If words pass between priest and driver, I'm not close enough to hear.

The priest stops walking.

The car stops moving.

The priest turns around, holds his hand up, the palm of prohibition foremost.

The confrontation is brief and long; it ends with the car slowly backing away until it slides off the footpath and joins the traffic in the roadway.

The priest, once more walking slowly, goes on reading his breviary.

York Road

Walking down York Road
making for Upper Rathmines
at the point where high hedges
give way to low walls
a man and a woman
come towards me, both stout,
middle-aged, well-hapt-up,
the man slightly ahead,
they used to be called tinkers,
the woman's hair still fair,
that glorious distinctive shade.

Today the three of us
are alone in the road.

The man and I exchange
perfunctory greetings
but the woman stops me:
'Do you like apples?' she says,
offering a brown-paper bag
with two big red apples in it
impaling me on the horns
of a truth-teller's dilemma
for I never liked biting
apples and much less now,

but to tell her the truth —
would be unforgivably rude.
Besides, what would Martin
Buber think of me?

So I tell a happy lie —
my mother turning in her grave,
my father dancing in his —
and thank the kind woman,

and she and I exchange
heartfelt good wishes, and part.

What a Young Man Said to My Mother

1

On the few occasions Maurice came back to Findrum with me after closing time I always made sure to be up in good time the next morning to get him out and away before my mother got up.

She was intelligent, she was charming, she was the best of company, but she was also deeply puritanical; and she always got up at seven on the dot.

My bedroom looked out on the back garden. It was divided by a thin partition from the kitchen, which looked out on the front garden.

2

One morning I woke up too late. No sign of Maurice. I looked at my watch: a quarter past seven. I got the smell of breakfast from the kitchen and heard the sound of voices. My mother and Maurice amicably conversing? Maurice too could charm the birds from the trees. But my mother was no bird.

I dressed in haste and trepidation, listening all the time. I couldn't make out more than the occasional commonplace word or two. Then, soaring out as clear as a bell in Maurice's full-throated Munster voice, one sentence: 'Mrs Hutchinson, one kiss from Pearse's mouth means more to me than all the women in the world.'

3

Several things happened me at one and the same time: I waited for my mother to read the riot act or have a heart attack; I exulted that someone I loved could so bravely declare his love for me; and I hoped that, despite his Munster charm, he truly meant it — or, at least, wasn't exaggerating too much.

I braced myself and faced into the kitchen, putting on as nonchalant an air as possible. My mother put my breakfast in front of me as I sat down. Maurice was tucking in without the faintest sign of a hangover. They went on chatting sporadically in the most 'normal' fashion, with me joining in once or twice. You'd have thought those two — in various ways my nearest and dearest — had known each other for years.

I managed to finish my breakfast without mishap. My mother got up to do the dishes. Maurice offered to dry them. She accepted. I went up to the bathroom.

4

By the time I came down again she'd gone out to Mass in the Three Patrons. Maurice and I chatted for a while, then I left a brief note on the hall table and we went down town. My mother and Maurice never met again.

Tuning Fork Chair-leg

A well-planted Munsterman in the prime of celibate life
at the top of an outsize classroom where
he'd managed to marshal a couple of hundred boys
with a tuning fork on the empty desk beside him
he was the monarch of all he surveyed —

Music his mission how could so great a school
survive a second longer without a choir?
His black soutane swirling with passionate love —
Bernini's Teresa had nothing on him —
he drew from its folds the leg of a wooden chair to show he
  meant business
that leg was as blonde and as wavy as his own fine-head-of-hair
avenging and bright he brandished it high
then stowed it away again deep in the dingy crevasses
we hoped for ever but knew in our bones
the first boy to audition sang like an angel
not avenging just bright
he was into the choir with a pat on the head like a shot

The next few were passable. One boy, though,
got biffed three times on the hand with the chair-leg
squirming back to his desk drained, undone
the leather we twigged was benign by comparison. And why?
Because he couldn't sing and not to be able to sing was a sin
in the eyes of that man who loved music so much

I knew I couldn't sing not even, as now, to save my life
so I sat there and trembled in secret, already undone
or so I thought until at last it was really my turn
to ascend the scaffold the tuning fork twanged out in menace
I did my despairing best —

But it wasn't just not good enough it was far and away the worst
he towered above me hard handsome avenging and brilliant
he demanded my right hand and gave it six
it fell to my side, feeling crippled
I hirpled back to my desk, undone
half my body numb
the hand was useless for — no I can't remember how long
does it matter? but no bones were broken and that was a miracle
does it matter? but I wish I could
how many other boys or whether
that choir ever happened but this much I know:
next morning in our class we looked at our own brother, Guk,
with something approaching relief although it was said
he'd kicked a boy once down the stairs but not long after
the chair-leg-and-tuning-fork festival you'd have to
feel sorry for his musical ears how much we must have hurt them
he was transferred back to his native haunts
God help those poor boys though who knows —
Perhaps he transferred his love to a different art:
the painting of still lives —
The Hand of a Painter Manqué, with Tuning Fork and Chair-leg

On a Summer Day in West Cork

for Robert Welch

On the top of Coom
one burning midsummer day
a boy of ten or twelve, with sunburnt hair,
stript to the waist for the great heat,
brings us our black pints frothing like elderflowers
and wild but welcoming
for lack of a sandwich to serve us
breaks two eggs on the roof of the car to fry in the sun
and in minutes they're done —
though in that small while I have counted three times
the teats of a sow that was pottering about
on the top of Coom
that broiling midsummer afternoon
and each time it comes out as eleven.

Names

Many medicines have dull, awkward, ugly names. Which isn't the point, but you can't help noticing . . .

When the doctor said he'd put me on antibiotics, I thought nothing of it — except to hope.

So the minute I got those particular tablets the name delighted me: *Clavamel.* A clean, crisp sort of a name.

Nearly my favourite word in the whole world is: *Clavel.* The Spanish word for carnation.

Now *clavamel* contains *clavel* and if you take *clavel* out of *clavamel* you're left with: *Am.* Which was the first name of Am Bedkar, who was the leader of the 'Untouchables' and raised them up off their knees.

And when India was at last independent Nehru went to see Gandhi and asked him: 'Who shall I ask to write our Constitution?'

And Gandhi said: 'Am Bedkar.'

And Nehru did as Gandhi advised, and Am Bedkar said 'yes' and wrote it.

Triana

In Triana, the gypsy quarter
across the broad river from Seville,
part of yet apart from
that proud non-gypsy city,
the hottest place in Europe,
the small houses were all blazing blinding white —
the whitest houses in Europe, even in Spain —

And the first street-name I saw,
landing from the long, broad bridge, was
PUREZA
meaning purity in blazing sky-blue letters,
a deep rich blue echoing the intense blue
of that most southern sky, a blue never in the north
seen or even imagined,
every letter clear, strong, upstanding
CLEAR
as perfect as any craft in all the proud north
of Spain itself or Europe.

And turning a corner I saw
another vision, a tiny girl —
la morenita in person —
a dark south-Indian face and blazing black eyes
and curling blue-black hair, in a snow-white dress
with a flaring skirt, gold sleepers glinting
in her tiny ears as she danced,
bare arms tapering high with castanets,
dextrous and musical as an olive grove alive with cicadas
and in the next street another like her
and then another —
and not a single grown-up showed.

Just three or four very small
and very lovely girls

dancing immaculate in siesta time.
And not one begged
or spoke.

Santarem

Alcobaça
Batalha
Queluz
Tomar
through a springtime landscape like a Tuscan background —
then suddenly the young traveller finds himself
in Santarem with just about enough cash
for a cheap glass of green wine — and the very first bar
he comes to looks right he squeezes in
to a half-space at a crammed counter;
a tall man next to him contrives to move up a little,
they slip easily into chatting, just enough
Portuguese and just enough English.
A friendliness grows.
His name is Manuel Pinto.
'I'm a gypsy,' he says — no swaggering,
just stating a fact.

The young man asks:
'Where's the best place in Santarem
to hitch a lift from back to Lisbon?'
His new friend advises against it —
and for the train then 'Oh I see,
well, I'll lend you the fare
and enough for a glass in Lisbon,
now let's have one for the road, you've time.'

'How'll I get the money back to you?'
'You know the Torre de Belém? Well,
many of my family live just near there,
give it to any of them.'
He smiles again,
kindly, amused, self-assured.
Was there a farewell hug?

The young man, now an old man,
can't remember.

Days later, in the money,
he goes for perhaps the fifth time
to feast his eyes on the tower near the mouth of the river,
on its compact, buckled, squat, earth-hugging, non-Gothic
  beauty,
squat and perfectly itself like an old Adler,
then calls at the nearest house —
and was he at least half-expecting
who knows what adventure,
a gypsy party, music flamenco or Balkan,
but deep down what most he was hoping
was Manuel Pinto himself to be there by some miracle.

But they're not called Pinto, they know of no Pintos,
the same at the next house,
the same at the third,
at the fourth door no answer —
so the young man gives up
and goes away to raise a lonely glass.

The Scent of Memory

1

Walking up South King Street with a Trinidadian friend, heading for Grafton Street, then Davy Byrne's, I was twenty-one-or-two and he was three years younger. It was five-to-eight as we passed the Gaiety and a swanky first-night woman swept into the theatre through the swing doors nearly grazing us but leaving in the street air around us, and in our heads for minutes, a strong haze of perfume. My friend stopped, looked after her briefly, then as we walked on he said: 'That scent reminds me of a Portuguese lad I made love to at the back of the racetrack in Port-of-Spain.' He smiled at the memory.

2

I'd already learnt that in Trinidad Portuguese meant Brazilian.

3

I couldn't help wondering whether, after the pubs closed that night, I'd be as lucky as that Portuguese or Brazilian lad. It was a whole week for Christ's sake since I'd had to leave my friend's digs before seven in the morning. Seven was when his landlady, Miss Ward, a native speaker from Donegal, got up. She was kindly, but there are limits.

4

When I asked him to name the scent he couldn't. But he recognized it, and remembered the pleasure, and the one who'd shared it.

5

'Pearse is very lonely when Bert's away,' said Miss Ward to one of his fellow-boarders, who told him, who told me.

All Four Letters of It

i.m. Bert Achong (1930-1998)

I wrote your name in snow
on the Capuzinerberg

clear blue sky
bright winter light

I wrote your name
on a high hill

remembering long
delight new-lost

I wrote your name in snow

Doorways

The smell of poverty such as I hadn't known it
for half-a-century struck me as soon as I opened the door.
'Hold on,' I said, 'I'll see what I can do.'
The engulfing stench of deep-down poverty.

A man in his late thirties — early forties? —
he'd been calling for two or three years,
once or twice a month. And always clean.
Never like that.
Never before at all like that.

The very same dark, acrid stench
seeping out of the black doorways
of York Street and Gardiner Street when I was young
in the '40s and '50s, that black was not
the beautiful black of living limbs and faces
but a dull, dense black, despair devouring —
great hunger devouring the only thing it can
devour: hope.

A fortnight later the poor man came again.
Clean again. A new man.
But still in need. I gave him what I could,
then stayed at the half-open door
to watch him down the steps and down the path
and out the iron gate,
then closed and locked my door.

Near the Grand Canal

for Patrick Galvin
'that gallant man'

1

Crossing a canal bridge, I walked along a terrace of two-storey houses. No steps up or down. Medium-sized front gardens.

It was a quiet afternoon. No one about.

Then, a few gardens ahead, a stocky man with a shock of springy grey hair came out the gate, preceded by a small white dog, which pitter-pattered away along the pavement, as if determined to go off on its own.

The man closed the gate carefully, then called after the dog: 'Connolly.' In a quiet tone of authority. No need to bark.

The dog trotted back to the man. Together they crossed the road. I watched them round a corner, still close together.

Connolly!

That name made my day.

Still does.

2

But I couldn't help thinking of that great half-lost cause James Connolly died for — and of all the other fine causes never entirely won, or entirely lost.

And then again I thought of the great beauty of Lily Connolly, his wife, when, not long before they killed him — and *he* was trying to console *her* — she cried out to him: 'But your beautiful life, James, your beautiful life!'

Basement Bar

She came down the stairs fast
a dark-haired woman, perhaps thirty,
and straight to the nearest table
sank on her knees before
an older woman sitting there
and cried out loud and clear
'You knew my lover, didn't you?'
in a voice brimming over with anguish.
The other woman stroked the dark hair.
If she spoke it was so quietly
nobody else could hear.

Just then my host came in
to bring me back home for supper.
I went — but paused at the turn of the stairs
for one more look at the woman
who spoke the name 'lover' so clear.

Andersonstown, Belfast 1974 / Dublin 2011

The Woman Who Chose Cakes

Ten men at an oblong table,
their weekly meeting in Ozanam House,
they sit in judgement on the needs of the poor.
A bookshop assistant aged eighteen
on a pound a week — the lion's share
goes to his mother — lets
his visiting comrade, seven years older —
they visit the poor in Corporation Buildings,
Corporation Street and Foley Street —
report their dealings and all is fine.

But now an older comrade
with doleful countenance relates
a shocking tale, a mother — how
a single mother long in receipt
of a half-crown voucher (the wonted bounty)
stopped at the small shop window
by one of her three small kids
devouring with his eyes the icing
white and blue on small cheap cakes
and he clamours his mother for cakes
and his siblings clamour as loud

and the mother can stand it no longer
and her heart goes out to them all
and she casts all prudence to the four wild winds
and to hell with the scrimping and scraping
and the long, long
                                        being beholden
and into the shop with her half-crown voucher
she blows it all on cakes cakes cakes.

Naming Water

Was it Whitby or Drogheda? When I walked at dawn from a central hotel to the soundless docks? I think it must have been Dundalk . . .

Big heaps of sand imported from Holland. Further on, a small ship or big boat, still asleep. Its name on the side in clear bold letters astonished me:

AGUA

The Spanish for water. As I stood there gazing with delight at this Dutch boat with a Spanish name (the flag looked Dutch), a sailor came up on deck. 'Dutch?' I said. He said yes.

'With a Spanish name!' He agreed enthusiastically, then said the name real loud, relishing the g, which he pronounced like a guttural *c* in Gaelic, only stronger.

I smiled and said, 'Tot siens', preparing to walk on. Surprised to hear himself told goodbye in his own language, he replied in it. I couldn't understand a word.

We waved at each other, he went back down again, I walked on through the morning once again quiet.

Remembering how the water sellers at the station in Seville, running along beside the train, called out *Agua! Agua!* in hoarse voices, pronouncing the *g* like a guttural *g* in Gaelic — a sound which, in Spanish, doesn't officially exist . . .

Shanty Towns near Barcelona

1

Sammy and I went walking with Gibson Cowan along a dirt-track through a sort of no-man's-land near a shanty town.

Some two hundred yards in from the track we saw a makeshift cross on which a dog had been hanged. Were there flies? If there were, time has driven them away. But I can see that long, off-white underbelly, and a few light-brownish, orange-ish markings on the limbs.

'Dirty-white' might be more accurate, but I jibbed at that.

2

On a different day Sammy and I, just the two of us, went walking along a different dirt-track towards a shanty town we'd been given vague directions to. After a while what looked like a settlement appeared on our left, a little distance away at the top of a stretch of rough ground — not too steep-looking.

Sammy was wearing her 'sensible' shoes, so the going was easy enough. At the top, on level ground, we faced a street — unpaved but still a real street, with low-roofed, adobe-style buildings on both sides. And all these by-no-means detached small dwellings were bluewashed — in a lovely shade of blue, halfway between dark and light. A blue that was, or seemed, both tranquil and spectacular. More intense than the Mediterranean sky.

And proud. Proclaiming a proud community? A signal of such pride, such possible pride, we'd already been enchanted by — and I mean almost literally — as soon as we'd reached the level ground. For there, on the broad end-wall of the settlement, we could read, in clear, bold, regular, perfectly painted, big white letters on the bluewash

PASEO DE LA PRIMAVERA

How on earth to translate that? Spring Walk? Or — why not? — Springtime Boulevard.

So Sammy and I walked the length of that boulevard, or walk. Some fourteen or fifteen dwellings. Two or three people came to their doors to greet us. Then we went back to the end, or beginning. There was a bar, with no chairs, tables, or stools. But a counter to lean on. And a man behind it, soberly but not shabbily dressed, who served us and had one with us when we pressed him to. Yes, he said, they were making out. But he didn't say how.

We shook hands and went down the slope. When we reached the dirt-track we looked back up. He'd already disappeared.

Mitteleuropa

Gautier called Spain the land of the unexpected
but was I at all expecting as I dined in style
in Joyce's favourite eating house in Zurich
to hear for the first time the name Vivaldi
on the lips of a 35-ish balding tubby
US corporal of Irish descent in love with a 23-year-old
fresh-faced springy-haired private of Slavic stock and then,
entrancingly hummed by the said corporal,
several minutes of music by the said Vivaldi,
and the very next day alighting on the platform at Salzburg
to read on the side of a white shed
impeccably painted in big black letters
WAITING ROOM FOR MOZART.

Green Window

The small kitchen in the attic scarcely had room for anything bar the big double bed. Which was surprisingly comfortable.

There was one small, square window above the sink. It was entirely covered — and very neatly too — by some very thin green material.

I was always amazed at how much light that green window let in. Chelsea light.

One forenoon, I asked him could he show me how to tie a Windsor knot. They were all the rage at the time. I'd tried myself, in vain. I didn't even like them: too blowzy. But, stupidly, I wouldn't be bested.

'I'm a dab hand at the Windsor knot,' he said. 'I'll show you all right.'

And he did. But not around my neck.

Valencia

1

Of all the Valencian wonders Juan unveiled
for Lorca's delectation when he visited
nothing pleased the poet more
than the big old magnolia tree in the park.

So he took me to the park to show me
what had so deeply moved Federico
and we stood there quietly, admiring.

But as I was praising the blossoms
Juan said that what thrilled Lorca most
was not the flowers but the roots.

They spread out all round, from the base
like dark gnarled fingers, claws,
reaching out, grasping, digging,
writhing like dark snakes.

I thought of Lorca's death
as if there was any connection
but as if there *was* some connection.

2

Next day I crossed a broad bridge
over the river Turia
and stopped halfway to lean
on the parapet looking down
in something like dread
at the driest of riverbeds
all that rugged uneven grey ground
absent water shrieking in the deep blue air

a great river the flow of life
killed by drought
writhing and repelling.
Nobody was trying to walk along it.

Matsudaira

I'd like to rhyme the Japanese clan Matsudaira
with the Catalan word *captaire*
meaning beggar, and it would rhyme too.

I want to rhyme *captaire*
with the Irish word *meidhre*
meaning merriment: well, wouldn't it?

Resistance

My father and mother when I was born called me
        Xan
My brother they named
        Mingos
but the mighty church and the civil powers —
most uncivil and far from ours —
when they held me over the font
could only muster
        Juan
and the best they could muster for him was of course
        Domingo
official imperial versions,
and so we were written down for ever in the parish register
but our father and mother and all the family
and everyone else in the village
and in all the hills around
kept on calling my brother
        Mingos
kept on calling me
        Xan

Sleepwalking 1

Sleeping in his armchair the sometime sleepwalker dreamt
he was waking up halfway down the top flight of stairs
but not walking or stepping but already sitting
on the middle stair of seven half way between
the top landing and the midway landing
apparently happily ensconced asleep there —
for how long already? — apparently entirely un-
afraid to find himself there in so
unexpected and conceivably menacing a situation
at three o'clock in the morning in the middle of the night.

After the Pageant

On the dark back steps of the town hall in Leeds
a Belfast girl speaking in bitter anger,
bitter and bleak: 'We don't exist' —
for on the lit-up stage inside
cravatted garrotted music had ushered in
a brisk historical pageant of old suffering
up to the '16 Rising, still apparently
glorious, then after the interval:
We go into Europe! Fanfare! Skirl!
as if between '16 and the Common Market
no Black-and-Tans, no Civil War, no pogroms,
no Civil Rights, Burntollet nor Long Kesh,
no torture — all that
suffering, her people's long suffering and hope
in a quarter-of-an-hour swept under the stage
or out the emergency exit: Eliminate
the negative — no wonder
that Belfast girl cried out:
'We don't exist!'

Moffat

The great ram of Moffat
up high on his plinth
his horns more regal than antlers
is monarch of all
the country around him
the wool and the wealth and the Duke of Buccleuch
a few steps away on this bleak winter day
the doors of that hotel wide open to the street
a huge and golden roaring fire embraces you.

At the foot of the plinth
in a small stone
half-moon basin
silver paper
trapped in black ice.

Light

1

It was a fine day in early July. A little after half-three. I wish I could remember the precise date but I can't. I was sitting in a favourite place, my back to the partition: reading and drinking and looking out through the big window on the opposite side of the front bar at the sky, the well-kept grey brick, the black wrought-iron balconies.

The door swung open, and in you came. I'd never seen you before. You walked right up to me and asked me was I me. I said I was. You asked me would I have another drink. I said I would. You went and got the drinks and sat beside me. We talked and talked.

2

Gradually the place filled up. I suggested we find somewhere quieter. You agreed and we went round the corner, into a somewhat larger pub. Apart from the barman we had it to ourselves.

We sat side by side, our backs to the wall. The venetian blinds were half-open, so the place was in a kind of half-light. We went on talking.

After a while I turned and looked straight at you: at the light in your eyes, and the light on your lips.

And that was the beginning of the best that ever happened me.

Milarepa

1

Brother and sister
kneeling side by side
on the one prie-dieu

He is seven
She's five

Her long hair
is golden
His long hair
turquoise

That's how Milarepa
recalls it much later
after centuries
of abnegation

Such merciless victories
over the self
they make the severest
christian ascetic
sybarite

2

At fifteen
he killed his mother
and fled far away
very slowly
becoming a saint

3

Glaciers later
he dared return
to the family home
the crime scene
all was in ruins
no board for sharing
prayer

Nightmare guilt
the implacable beauty
of grey

a spurning of sadness
even the deepest
all is homeless
bleak

He tells that visit
like a poet reporting
on Corcomroe
or the classical theatre
of Japan
all filmed by moonlight
or pitch-dark

But how well he remembers
the colours of childhood
even after
quenching not only
the vulgar flesh
but harder still
the pretentious soul

How well
he remembers
her long golden hair
his own turquoise

when he was seven
and she was five

In Praise of French

1

Jean Jaurès, the great Socialist leader who tried to stop the '14-'18 war and got killed for his pains, once said: *On appelle patois à la langue des vaincus*, meaning: The term 'patois' is applied to the language of the conquered.

That's one in the eye for the conqueror . . .

2

Piaf, Brassens: the magnificent way they perform the magnificent sound of the letter *r*. Almost like the guttural *g* in Gaelic. The zest they put into it — and yet it's as natural as breathing.

Not to mention Jean Marais. The young film star? Maybe, but when he played the Beast in *La Belle et la Bête* what is unforgettable is the way he said, when he spied on the Beauty from his hiding place, 'Ma Rose'.

A hoarseness beyond all hoarseness. The French *r* at its most guttural, like the sound of the woodcock, which is the sound of the wood but even more the sound of the earth — not the sound of the planet of hills and skies but the sound of the soil itself, of the ground and the under-earth and all creatures on and under it — that guttural *r* drawn out, though not too much, and the vowel *o* drawn out, though not too far, and the *z* sound of the *s* — no three letter-sounds could have been put together more aptly or more completely to convey such deep longing, menace, despair — I can't believe that Marais ever gave a better performance than the way he uttered that one word, those three sounds . . .

Lakes in Leitrim

Once I had the lakes of Leitrim
all spread out on a big map
          under these two eyes
every single lake in Leitrim
and not even one overflowing.

But each one a blue pool
as rich a blue as mortal
          eye could see or god imagine —
mellow, young, and calm that blue,
no excess yet sensuous.

They came in all shapes and sizes
          but the only colour was blue
and only one shade of it —
ultramarine, let's hope.

Countless but not overcrowding
big lakes and small like pools
          of a blue more light than dark
yet vivider than light could be
and far more cool than south.

And all this clear calm warm blueness
on a ground of perfect white
          a whole snow county but as if
the snow was considerate —
could never invade blue.

I stood for all of ten minutes
gazing at the lakes of Leitrim
          all spread out before me
drinking my bright fill — and then
my friend bore me off in his car again

throughout the dark-green county —
bright after the heavy rains . . .

The Abbot of Piro

At the Meadow of Pigs in the centre of Ireland
she bought a chariot, rode it fast
till she reached the Ford of the Black Pool
where she bought a boat with a single sail
and putting the chariot into the boat she sailed
across the treacherous water safe to Wales.

Landing she lifted the chariot out of the boat —
she wasn't called Samson for nothing —
and putting the boat into the chariot
she rode it fast until she reached her forest:
she was again Abbot of Piro.

But after a while she tired of Abbacy,
the monks were too much like the world,
so leaving the boat behind she drove her chariot
to a nameless clearing in the forest where —
dismissing the chariot, telling it never to come back —
she lived eight years on watercress and cloudberries.

And there she settled, not far in from the shore,
for she was beginning to feel her age,
getting tired for example of lifting boats
into and out of chariots
and chariots out of and into boats,
not to mention blessing,
for blessing meant building,
meant building, specifically, churches —
admittedly not very big,
and the odd beehive cell.

She blessed more people than ever there,
she blessed the birds and animals,
she blessed byres and beehive cells,
the memory of one tin-miner,

the chariot and boat she no longer needed,
then last of all she blessed herself
and hirpled her way to the End of Earth.

Ruudi in Amsterdam

Handsome at twenty and nobody's fool
sitting directly under the bare bulb
his hair the exact rich colour
of a redsetter's coat
than which no red could be lovelier
he turned his face up
as if to be kissed,
then down again, in the nick of time
so the would-be kiss just barely grazed
his perhaps quite natural red hair.

Amsterdam 1971/Dublin 2010

Two Degrees

Any friend of Driscoll's is a friend of mine,
said Gottschalk. So look me up if you're ever in these parts.
With pleasure, said the caller. But where exactly?
In the German-English dictionary, said Gottschalk.

If you're a friend of Gottschalk's you're a friend of mine,
said Galifardeu. So look me up if you're ever in these parts.
With pleasure, said the caller. But where exactly?
In the Catalan-Irish dictionary, said Galifardeu.

Pipers and a Fiddler

'I play for the soul, not the feet,'
said the Clare piper Garret Barry.

Willie Clancy said in an interview:
'The Irish language is the greatest music of all.'

And when there was a piper in the company
the Leitrim fiddle player Joe 'Lacky' Gallagher always said:
'Let the piper lead.'

Merrion Square, 1948

I wandered away from the big party room, into a smaller empty room, closing the door between: suddenly the hubbub hushed.

At the far end of the smaller now bigger room I could see a small neat figure standing on a balcony with a brandy glass in his hand. I joined him.

We stood in silence side by side, looking down at the dark private greenery. Then I told him my name, offering my hand. He took it in a light grip, told me his name was Deesh.

'That's a lovely name,' I said, wanting to add 'for a lovely young man'. His features were neat and brown. He was an Indian medical student.

After another short silence he took out his glass eye, placed it between his snow-white teeth, and began to crunch.

That was the only sound in the still night square. I fled.

Sleepwalking 2

Sleepwalking
Sleep-falling
so here I am waking
stretched out full-length on the floor
and blood coming down my face from the hairline
fast and lavish down onto the skirting
and now I think I can still move so I rise
to my feet amazing without much trouble
and stand up straight as a rookie martinet

with blood pouring down from my brow
onto my lovely new shirt and onto the floor
I'm sopping it up with a hanky will the blood
never stop
cascading
the bump at the hairline still swelling
the pain is unceasing it's all but unbearable

I look down at my lovely new shirt
a present from Italy
blue and white stripes
the blue is a rich blue
the blue stripes are slightly
but only slightly
narrower than the white

I wore it for the first time yesterday
and kept it on even in bed
now it's all covered in blood
no not all but splashed
                                        haphazard

The beautiful damage is done
the blood is every bit as lovely as the shirt
how can my blood at my age

be so rich and glowing a red
the blood goes on
cascading
and I go on mopping it up
and gazing
in delight at such beauty
in *awe* at such beauty
in fear
          at the blood I'm losing
afraid of my own blood
Imagine being afraid of your own blood!
Especially when it's so beautiful

As I drop the new red hanky
white only minutes ago
onto the bloodstained floor
to hell with the floor
it's decrepit
                  threadbare
                                    mousy
and I'm resplendent, sixteen again
for my new shirt isn't blue and white anymore
it's blue and it's white and the richest of reds
but you can't wear for ever such beauty as that
So I hang the shirt up in the bathroom
and rinse my head
gingerly
             in cold water

It's 4 a.m. on the 2nd of August
Nineteen-Ninety-Seven
I think of you and how
only a few short hours from now
you'll be best-manning it in Central Park

truly young and truly resplendent
in your lovely new white suit

And all of a sudden the pain vanishes
completely
the blood-flow dwindles
to a trickle
then stops for good

Listening to Bach

Gottschalk,
said Driscoll,
why've you never finished that poem about angels?
Because,
said Gottschalk,
I was listening to Bach.

Letter to Kazantzakis

Some have accused me of writing
too much in celebration.

So many things, and people,
still left unpraised

and much still to mourn.

Still

On a warm sunny day in the summer
not to be able to go out:
that must be hell, a man thought.

On a warm sunny day in the summer
not to be able to go out:
that is hell, he knows.
(*1998*)

On a warm sunny day in the summer
to still be alive to look out
at the trees and grass and the sky:
that's not too bad, he thought,
that's not too far from heaven.
(*2000*)

Swans

A poet who was also a calligrapher
wanted to represent the new millennium
    so he painted in Indian ink
        (which he'd always loved)
            a swan
        followed by three circles
and showed it to everyone he knew
(which by that time wasn't many).
All but two wanted to know what it meant.
The circles were just as big as the swan
    so he painted a new picture:
        a swan
    followed by three circles,
only this time the swan was upper-case
    and the circles lower-case.
He thought the circles looked a bit like cygnets.
So he showed it to almost everyone he knew:
            Swan with three cygnets.
    But nobody recognized the circles.

        So he gave up
        for the time being
                and said:
I must live a lot longer
        or come back
in two thousand two hundred and 22.

On the Locker

On the locker-lid
a biscuit-wrapping
                                    torn,
waves in a sudden breeze
just like a flower.

Dictated to Michael O'Dea
in St James's Hospital
20/12/2011

Mistaking Cavafy

Mistaking Cavafy for Pessoa
in a magazine photo
may not be a hanging offence.

But taking a light-bulb reflected
in a window for the moon . . .
though even that would pale beside

mistaking the moon for a light-bulb —

which hasn't yet happened
so let us be thankful
for mercies great and small.

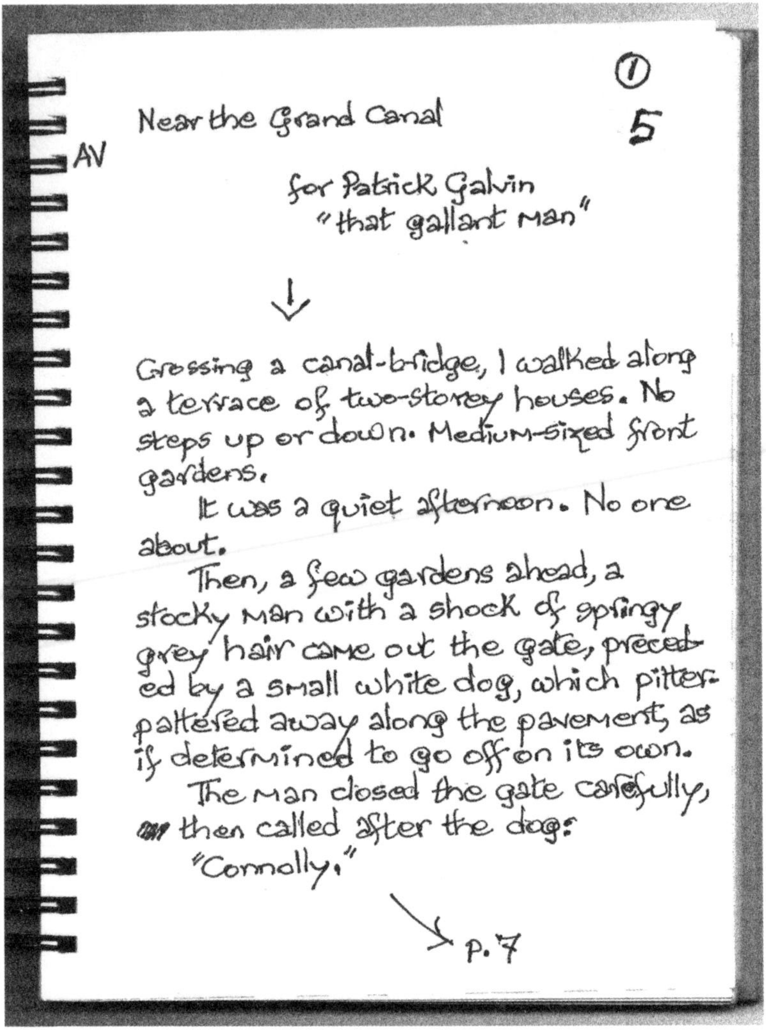

Near the Grand Canal

AV

①

5

for Patrick Galvin
"that gallant man"

↓

Crossing a canal-bridge, I walked along a terrace of two-storey houses. No steps up or down. Medium-sized front gardens.

It was a quiet afternoon. No one about.

Then, a few gardens ahead, a stocky man with a shock of springy grey hair came out the gate, preceded by a small white dog, which pitter-pattered away along the pavement, as if determined to go off on its own.

The man closed the gate carefully, then called after the dog:

"Connolly."

→ p. 7

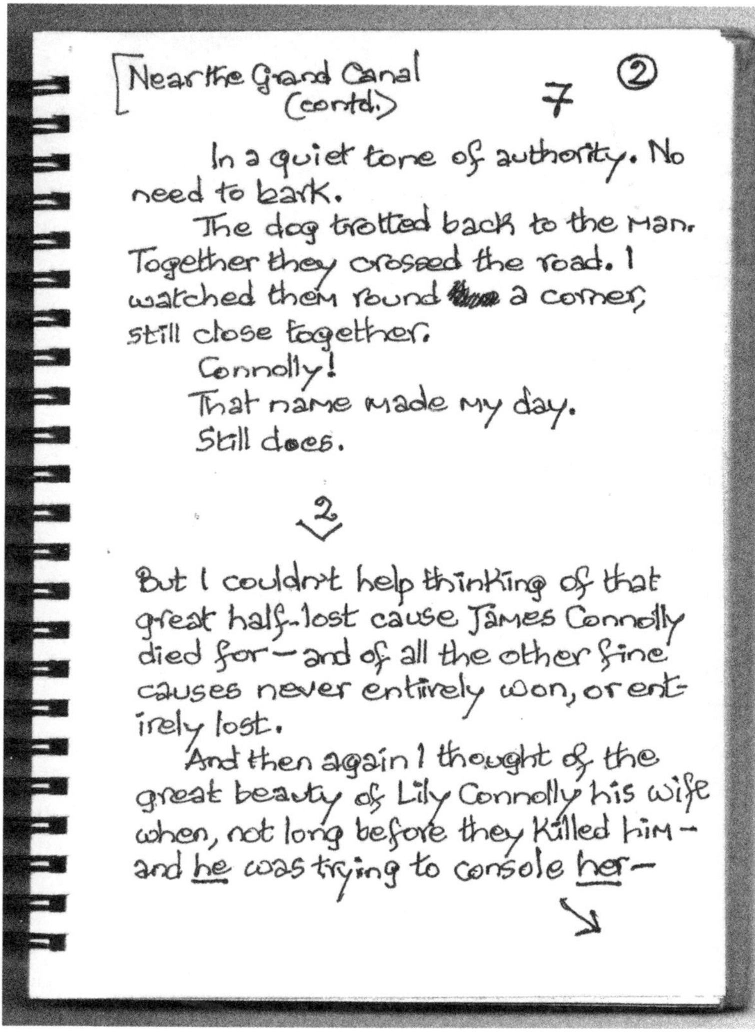

[Near the Grand Canal
(contd.)

7 ②

In a quiet tone of authority. No need to bark.

The dog trotted back to the man. Together they crossed the road. I watched them round a corner, still close together.

Connolly!

That name made my day.

Still does.

2

But I couldn't help thinking of that great half-lost cause James Connolly died for — and of all the other fine causes never entirely won, or entirely lost.

And then again I thought of the great beauty of Lily Connolly his wife when, not long before they killed him — and *he* was trying to console *her* —

↘

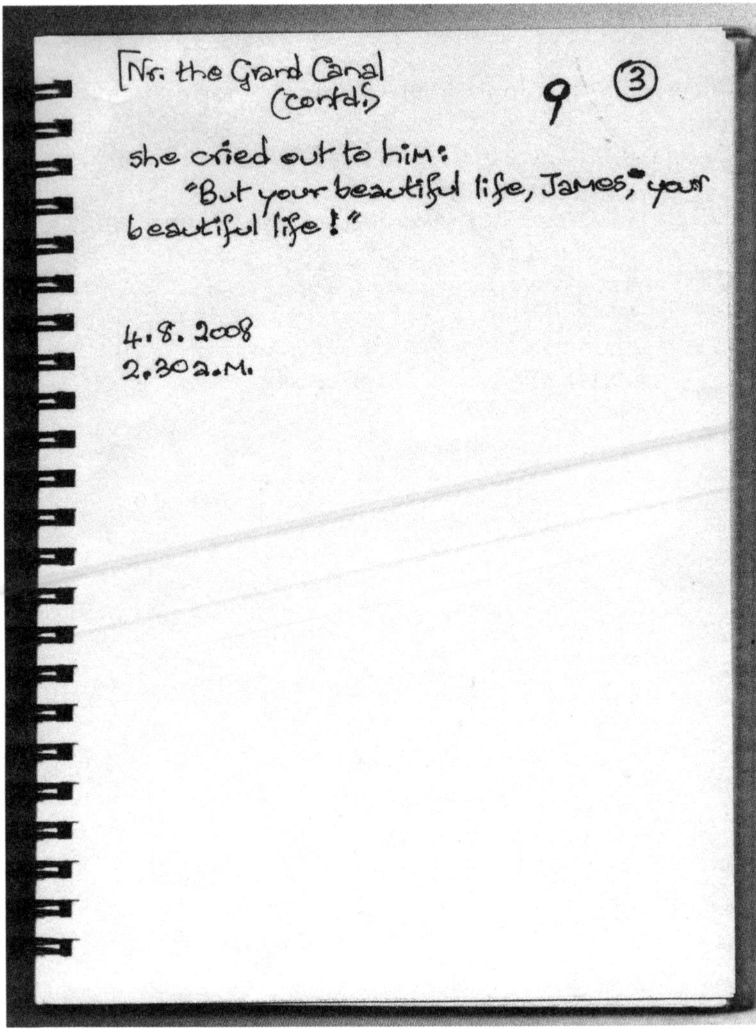
[Nr. the Grand Canal
(contd.)

9 ③

she cried out to him:
"But your beautiful life, James," your beautiful life!"

4.8.2008
2.30 a.M.

Acknowledgements

The epigraph 'He donat la meva vida al amor dels amics' was said to Pearse by Josep Queralt i Clapes, co-founder during the Republic of the Catalan publishing house called Proa.

Some of these poems appeared in *Boulevard Magenta, Cyphers* and *Poetry Ireland Review*.

The Gallery Press acknowledges, with thanks, the contribution of Eiléan Ní Chuilleanáin and Vincent Woods to the preparation of this book and acknowledges also the Pearse Hutchinson Archive at NUI Maynooth for permission to reproduce pages from the poet's notebooks.